Introduction

The Equal Pay Act is not working. The gap between the average male and average female wage is actually widening. Few women are using the law successfully – in 1981 only six of the equal pay cases heard by industrial tribunals were successful. The Act, which was implemented in 1975, was not designed to tackle the two major obstacles facing women in paid employment – job segregation and low pay. All this calls for a *workable* amendment on equal value to be incorporated into the Equal Pay Act.

The book looks at why equal value is such an important concept for women's equality. Chapters deal with the low-pay trap and job-segregation, how skill is defined and why women's jobs are usually valued less than men's. Practical exercises, examples and discussion points encourage readers to question the assumption that 'male' skills should be more highly rewarded than 'female' skills. Separate chapters look at the role of the union; the Equal Pay Act; how job evaluation schemes work and Positive Action.

There are examples of equal value cases in other countries and their impact on women's pay in those countries. Three pairs of 'female' and 'male' jobs are then compared – a school cook and a dustman, a nursery nurse and a car mechanic, and a housewife and a managing-director. In each case the man earns more than the woman, even though a school cook is on a higher grade than a dustman.

A 'do-it-yourself' evaluation encourages women to compare the value of their work and their pay with male colleagues. An exercise on equal value has been prepared for groups who would like to try using 'role-play' as a way of learning.

The book is designed for use in women's groups, trade union courses, colleges of further education and schools. Each section has suggestions for group discussion and some practical exercises. The whole book could form the basis of a term's course or, alternatively, each chapter can be taken on its own.

For those particularly interested in equal pay for work of equal value, Chapters 7, 8, 9, 11 and 12 will be a useful source of information.

Groups using the do-it-yourself evaluation (chapter 11) or the role play exercise (chapter 12) would gain more if they have read most of the book. Both exercises need adequate preparation by the group leader/teacher.

THE Low Pay

This section gives some of the reasons why so many women are in jobs which are traditionally low paid, of low status and lacking in opportunity. You will no doubt be able to think of more reasons from your own experience.

JOB SEGREGATION

This is a term often used for something we can see in most workplaces. There are whole areas of work which are considered to be 'women's work' and they correspond to the lowest paid jobs. Women working in catering, cleaning or offices are at the bottom of the ladder of low paid workers, often doing the jobs which men have traditionally refused to do. For years employers have regarded these women as a legitimate source of cheap labour; low paid men have, by and large, organised themselves better.

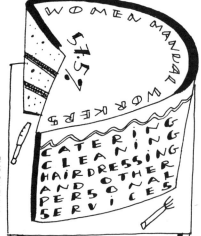

Women manual workers are concentrated in low paid jobs

WOMEN'S JOBS AND MEN'S JOBS

The majority of women work with other women in traditionally female industries – for example, light electrical engineering or textiles. Because historically women have been lower paid than men, these 'women only' workforces tend to be particularly poorly paid. The Equal Pay Act enables a woman to claim equal pay only with a man who is doing the same or broadly similar work in the *same workplace*. So these women are caught in a low pay trap; not only are they badly paid but there are no men with whom they can claim equal pay!

TOP JOBS FOR MEN ONLY

In most workplaces you will find there are more women at the bottom of the career structure. Men are more likely to rise to supervisory or management positions. For example, teachers have had equal pay since 1963 but more men than women reach the top of the profession. In secondary schools, 58% of all teachers on the lowest grade are women. But only 17% of all headteachers are women!

A DOUBLE LIFE

As many as 86% of all part-time workers are women. The reason most of these women work part-time is because they have to fit paid work in with their other job in the home. It is mainly women who stay at home to look after children, the elderly or sick (and sometimes the husband as well!). Single women looking after aged parents are expected to do two jobs and, like single parents, are often forced into *part-time* employment although they can ill afford it.

PRACTICAL EXERCISE
Make a list of employees in your immediate workplace, factory or office. If you are at school or college, list your teachers. Now rank them in order of seniority and see whether the proportion of women in managerial/supervisory positions is the same as the overall proportion of women to men in the workplace.

TRAP

"I don't like coming home to all the housework. My husband's prepared to help to a certain extent but my mum makes all the cakes for me. He got fed up with me working at Peek Frean's. I didn't mind it but he hated me going out and then coming back at 10 p.m."

"My husband and son don't lift a finger. When I worked full-time my husband wouldn't come in at all sometimes – even when I had cooked the dinner."

"My husband doesn't mind me working as long as the house is kept nice. It's very important to have his dinner on the table in time."

"I'm out of the house before six. Then I come home in the tea break at seven-thirty and wake them for school."

"If you need the money to keep the house going you have to work. I don't mind the work, but I'd like a more interesting job. A cleaning job is just like being at home."

BACK TO WORK

Women who have children often have to drop out of the job market and, when they are ready for work again, are unable to use their skills – either because they haven't kept up with new developments or because there aren't adequate child-care facilities.

"I'd like to work with handicapped kids and I'd go to college to train if they had a creche." *Bar Assistant*

"I don't like the job, no. But it's the hours that suit. I could have gone back to the bank for a few hours each day, but I didn't want to leave the baby. Now I'm at work in the evenings, my husband can do it. I think my qualifications (five 'O'-levels) were used at the bank. I really enjoyed it. It wasn't boring. There should be more facilities for children at work and then you could

take them with you and have lunch with them." *Evening Contract Cleaner*

"I'd like to go back to being a computer tape operator but there's the problem of the school holidays." *School Meals Supervisor*

STARTING EARLY

At home and at school, girls are still prepared for a future in the home – primarily as housewives and mothers. In fact, they grow up to find they want to do interesting work but often have not got the right skills or qualifications.

More boys than girls do science and technical subjects at school or university. They are also prepared for technical jobs by helping dad at home. Far more men than women go into industry and commerce. Of all the apprenticeships in 1977, women got only 14% – most of these in hairdressing.

Most girls concentrate on literature and arts subjects at school. In post-school training and degree courses, a large number of girls go into teacher training for a career, which is contracting due to Government cuts, and into secretarial courses, which are being undermined by word processors and the micro-chip.

Teaching materials at schools reinforce this. Most reading books in primary

schools still show fathers and sons playing football, while girls passively watch or help mother in the kitchen.

At school, girls tend to be channelled into 'female' subjects e.g. home economics, while boys are more likely to do science e.g. design and technology.

CHRISTINE ROCHE

```
TECH.        TECH
SCIENCE      SCIENCE
TECH.        TECH
SCIENCE      LIT
TECH         LANG
SCIENCE      ART
TECH         LIT
SCIENCE      LANG
TECH         ART
SCIENCE      LIT
TECH         LANG
SCIENCE      ART
TECH         LIT
SCIENCE      LANG
LIT          ART
LANG         LIT
ART          LANG.
```

DISCUSSION POINTS

Do you know of, or can you find, any reading books for young children which show men doing housework or looking after babies and girls playing football?

Given a free choice, which subjects would you have liked to have studied at school? Which were you not given the opportunity to try and why?

If you have children, are there any differences between the subjects which your son(s) and daughter(s) study?

What were your main considerations when you took your present (or last) job?

If you have children compare your list with a member of the opposite sex.

What's the Job

Before reading this page, make a list of five jobs which you think are not paid as much as they should be. (If you don't know exactly how much jobs are paid, make a list of jobs which you *think* are the lowest paid.)

How many of the jobs are done usually by men, usually by women, or by both men and women?

VALUE: IT'S THE JOB – NOT WHO DOES IT

It is generally agreed that jobs should be evaluated according to the skill, effort (physical and mental), responsibility and working conditions required to perform them. But this is usually not what happens. The work that women do is likely to be given lower value than men's work for reasons that have nothing to do with any of these factors.

A typist, for example, may do similar work to a typesetter (who sets up the print for books and newspapers). But typesetters (predominantly male) are better paid than typists (usually women).

A childminder is considered unskilled, yet she takes the whole responsibility for children, combining the job of nurse, teacher and parent.

Cleaning is an unskilled job although it can involve elements required of a skilled job – use of hand and power tools (vacuum cleaners, washing machines), use of chemicals (bleach, detergents) and taking decisions.

HOW IS YOUR JOB LABELLED?

Sometimes job titles can make unskilled jobs seem more skilled than they really are. For example, Jane is a *cleaner* in a chemical firm but she thinks she should be paid the same as the (male) *hygiene officer* who does much the same work.

Attaching the label 'skilled' or 'unskilled' often has little to do with the actual job content. It may be in the employer's interest to define a job as unskilled or semi-skilled because the corresponding pay will be lower. It will be in a union's interest to define a job as skilled – even when technology has so changed the job content that it would not now be seen as skilled. Women, who are less unionised than men, are less likely to be defined as skilled workers even when their work requires the same amount of skill as their skilled, male colleagues.

Why We Don't Value Women's Work

*After the industrial revolution, women's work was seen to be more and more confined to the home and family.

*The concept of the family wage – where a man's wage is supposed to support the whole family – was used to pay women less.

*Poor bargaining strength and male domination of the unions.

*Childcare and home responsibilities.

WOMEN ARE OFTEN PAID LESS THAN THEY'RE WORTH

Women who work in the electrical components industry (a predominantly female occupation) use considerable manual dexterity, but are on lower grades than men lifting the boxes of finished products. Similarly, an up-market confectionery firm pays the male dough makers more than the women who ice and decorate the sweets. The grade and pay of the women reflect not the skill involved in their jobs but the traditional relationship between men's and women's pay.

Whole areas of women's work are undervalued, especially in the caring professions. The qualities and skills needed to nurse a sick person, look after a child, keep a house clean are regarded as *inherent* attributes in girls and women, not as *acquired* skills. The responsibility and skill of a nurse, home help and childminder are considerable yet they are not paid nearly as much as the job might be paid if it had traditionally been done by men. What's more, where some men do traditionally female jobs such as nursing, they get paid women's rates — and so earn far less than if they had gone into a more normal male job with the same level of responsibility and skill.

WHAT'S WRONG WITH THE EQUAL PAY ACT?

The 1975 Equal Pay Act made it unlawful for employers to pay a woman less than a man doing the same or broadly similar work in the same workplace (see Chapter 4). All women who have taken equal pay cases to an industrial tribunal have had to find a man with whom to compare themselves. Many women have not won their cases because they could not convince the tribunal that they were doing the same ('like') work as a man.

The Equal Pay Act has benefited some individual women who have taken cases to an industrial tribunal. But it has done nothing to help the majority of women who are trapped in low paid, female-dominated jobs. Women in these kinds of jobs – such as home helps and secretaries – are not able to compare themselves to men doing the same or similar work because men *don't* do them. If they did, you can be sure that the jobs would be more highly esteemed and better paid!

So even if all women doing the same or similar work as men won equal pay, women's average hourly pay would *still* be considerably less than men's – because of the *type* of work women do.

If you compare typical 'male' and 'female' jobs you will often find that the work the women are doing is as demanding or needs equivalent skills or experience as the male jobs but is paid at a lower rate *because* it is considered 'women's work'.

WORTH?

Shulton (GB) Ltd. in Whitley Bay has 200 employees. For a 36 hour week (in 1983) the company pays the porters £84.42 per week (one grade only). For the same hours a canteen workers gets £77.56 with a higher grade which rises to £81.80 per week, still £2.62 less than all porters. Why, in your view, do the porters earn nearly £7 per week more than canteen workers?

In a Midlands pottery factory the men 'threw' the plates and then gave them to the women who decorated them. The men were paid a higher basic rate than the women. Do you think that was fair? Who had the heaviest work and who had the most intricate work? Is one job more skilled than the other?

MAGGIE MURRAY/FORMAT

PRACTICAL EXERCISES

*Look at the illustration of the nurse and computer engineer p18. What criteria would you use to decide which job was the most valuable (e.g. responsibility, stress, training, physical strength)? Do you think that the pay of nurses and computer engineers accurately reflect their value?

*List some more female jobs and ask a man how much he would expect to be paid for doing them. Would he expect to be paid more than the women get?

DISCUSSION POINTS

Discuss why you think women's jobs are undervalued. Some ideas are in the box 'Why Are Women's Jobs Undervalued?'

Do we value skills which women use in the home (e.g. cleaning and childcare) less than skills which are taught to people after they leave school?

Discuss the different sorts of skills and responsibilities involved in looking after a 3 year old at home and driving a lorry.

Women IN

Workers in the last century joined together in unions to negotiate better wages and conditions with their employers. A group acting together (or collectively) is stronger than individuals who have to approach their employer separately. Traditionally men have joined unions in larger numbers than women. But in recent years much of the growth in union membership has come from women and, as a result, the voice of women has become much stronger within the trade union movement.

Over the last decade the unions have had to respond to the demands of women more and more. A number of unions have recognised that there are problems which they need to tackle and it is of fundamental importance to women in paid employment that unions are beginning to take more seriously issues which particularly concern women – such as part-time working, maternity rights and childcare and sexual harassment at work.

It is easy to find fault with large organisations like trade unions but the most important point to remember is that trade unions have been by far the most important factor in women winning equal pay battles. With legislation as an impetus, unions have been in a position to negotiate effectively for equal pay. Only a tiny minority of women take – and win – their equal pay claims in an industrial tribunal. And where women do take a case to the tribunal they stand a far better chance of winning if they have the legal and financial backing of their union.

Before reading the rest of this chapter, make a list of the advantages for women who join a union. Then make a list of reasons why you think women are less active than men in unions. Use the following points for discussion.

Women's TUC

SHEILA GREY/FORMAT

WHY WOMEN DON'T HAVE EQUAL UNION STRENGTH

These are some of the difficulties which women trade unionists face. In your discussion, you will probably explore some of the problems which we come back to in the section on Positive Action.

THE PROBLEMS

*Smaller workplaces: More women work in small workplaces than men. Small workplaces are less likely to be unionised. Employers can make their employees feel they are being 'disloyal' to join the union, or employees can feel that the union is irrelevant.

*Women work in less skilled sectors: Workers who require less training and experience can easily be replaced if they insist on a better deal. Because they tend to work in the sectors regarded as less skilled, women are particularly vulnerable to undercutting, redundancy and replacement by agency and temporary workers.

*Part-time work: Practically all part-time workers are women. Unionisation is particularly difficult among part-timers; wages are low so union dues seem high. Part-timers are often more isolated, don't know workers on other shifts and can't get to union meetings. Many unions have failed to recruit part-timers and take up the issues facing part-time workers with young children.

*Length of service: Home responsibilities mean women enter and leave the workforce more often than men. Joining a union seems pointless.

*Unions and the Media: Women who do not work in traditionally unionised industries may have their ideas of unions formed through the media. They may see unions as not relevant to their needs and only in terms of being told to go on strike. They may not understand that union membership can bring many advantages – for example, better pay or holidays through negotiations.

*Less economic power: Low paid women often lack real power. Clerks and cleaners cannot cause the same disruption as steel workers and miners and can more easily be replaced.

*A triple shift: Many women are already doing two full-time jobs – at work and at home. Children make evening meetings almost impossible. The TUC has recommended that branch meetings are held during working hours without loss of pay. But to get this requires a strong union – a Catch 22 situation.

*Unions are a 'man's world':
"When I'm with men, I don't have as much to say as when there are all women, because I don't want to be ridiculed by a man. They tend to make fun of you." *(Angie, TGWU)*

"My husband is in the union, but he hates me being active. He calls me the shop stupid." *(Bev, APEX)*

"A lot of women feel that the union is still predominantly a man's world, and that it takes a very strong-willed woman to encroach on it." *(May, APEX)*

HE UNIONS

When NUPE asked its branch district committees why they thought women's occupations were under-represented, the men blamed apathy or lack of union-mindedness. Women on a shop stewards course had very different ideas. Some were:

● **Structure of meetings is formal and confusing.**
● **Male reps don't understand women's problems.**
● **Women lack confidence.**
● **Women are intimidated on courses.**

In other words, there is something very subtle at work. Trade unions have many unspoken rules that make it difficult for women to feel comfortable. For example, speaking at a meeting takes a lot of courage. The men have had practice at it – at school, at home, in the union. They are surrounded by other male voices. It's a whole new ball game for women. Some comments from women:

"In our job, we are always the poor relation. It's our own fault because many don't belong or make themselves heard. Still, even then we don't get the support." *(Union Member)*

"Women aren't recognised as much as men. They haven't followed up on the protective clothing for instance. I've never seen our rep. No one ever pays attention to part-time workers." *(GLC Cleaner)*

"I've not been to a meeting for ages. If there is an afternoon meeting, we have to skip shopping. It's hard to find a time that is right for women." *(Clerk/Typist, London)*

CHRISTINE ROCHE

The Way Forward

Women have much to gain from trade unions. Although female membership is increasing, there are still too few women shop stewards, branch and district officers, full-time officials and executive committee members. Neither the first nor third largest unions – the Transport & General Workers and the General, Municipal & Boilermakers – have a single woman on their 39 and 40 member executives.

As women are more adequately represented in the hierarchy, at both national and branch level, unions will become increasingly sensitive to issues which particularly affect women – low pay, maternity leave, workplace creches and equal pay. The TUC Charter 'Equality For Women Within Trade Unions' (see p27) gives some ideas on how the union structure can better accommodate and encourage women in the trade union movement.

DISCUSSION POINTS
Do you think women earn less than men because they are not strongly organised in trade unions or because they do different sorts of jobs?

How can women influence the unions and have more say in the issues unions take up?

CHRISTINE ROCHE

HOW TO CLAIM

A woman who thinks she should have equal pay with a man should first ask her trade union to negotiate on her behalf. If this is unsuccessful and she wants to challenge the legality of her unequal pay, she must take her case to an industrial tribunal. It is important that she asks her union to give her legal advice and representation during this process as her employer will have considerable resources to argue his case. If a woman is not a member of a union, she could approach either the National Council for Civil Liberties or the Equal Opportunities Commission for legal backing.

There are four circumstances in which a woman can take an equal pay claim to an industrial tribunal:

1. if she does exactly the same job as a man who works for the same employer ('like work').

2. if she does work which is 'broadly similar' to a man's and any differences are not important.

3. if she does work which has been given an equal rating in a job evaluation study.

4. if she considers her work of equal value to a man's, she may make a claim under new regulations which come into effect in January 1984.

'LIKE WORK' AND 'BROADLY SIMILAR WORK'

A woman can claim to be paid the same as a man who is doing work which is the same as or broadly similar to hers. This has helped some women but the scope of the Act is very limited, for two main reasons. Firstly, opinions as to when work is broadly similar can vary widely. In one case, women in a warehouse were paid less than the men. The Court of Appeal found that their work was not similar because the women handled parcels that were lighter than those handled by the men.

The second problem with this provision is job segregation. A great many women work in 'women only' jobs, or are all in the bottom grade of mixed jobs. In these situations, it is impossible for a woman to find a man to compare herself with. Many cases taken before an industrial tribunal have failed because they cannot prove 'like work'. In one case, a community worker (a woman) was in charge of a male adventure playground worker. Although he was responsible to the community worker, the man was paid more. The community worker claimed equal pay but the tribunal dismissed her claim on the grounds that she was not engaged in 'like work' with the man as she had *more* duties and responsibilities!

Equal Pay

In the Republic of Ireland equal pay claims have a 92% success rate – due in part to women being able to claim equal pay for like work as well as equal pay for work of *equal value*. This makes it easier for a woman to bring a successful case.

In many cases, the problem for women is not so much that they are paid less than men in the same grade, as that the gaps between their grade and the grades above are disproportionately large. In one case, this was openly acknowledged by the Employment Appeals Tribunal. The judge there remarked that there was no doubt that the pay of the women applicants was discriminatory, since it was so much less than the men in the grade above. Although the women were not doing the same work as the men, their pay should not have been as low as it was. But because the work was different, there was no legal remedy. Tribunals cannot adjust disproportionate differentials.

DIFFERENT WORK GIVEN AN AN EQUAL RATING

Women can claim equal pay for work which has been given the same value as men's jobs under a job evaluation study. Employers are under no obligation to institute such schemes. Even where they do, the criteria may be biased (often unconsciously) to benefit men more than women. The values attributed to different qualities may simply reflect the fact that certain jobs have been paid less in the past, or that women have been prepared to work for less. Once a scheme has been instituted, the tribunal cannot question the values attached. This is why it is important for a trade union to be involved in the job evaluation exercise from the very beginning and for women to be fully represented on any consultative or decision-making committee.

Even a fair job evaluation system may not help all that much. It may not touch disproportionately large differences between the rates of pay of different grades.

From 1984 new regulations will allow a woman to claim equal pay for work of equal value. (See p.17 for details of the regulations.)

WHEN YOU CAN'T GET EQUAL PAY

The Act allows an employer to pay a man and a woman different amounts if the employer can show there is a *genuine material difference* between the two employees.

For example, a man may have been employed in the job longer, or may have been rated on merit as more worthy. Merit ratings may be particularly subjective and benefit more men than women.

OTHER OBSTACLES

1. There is no legal aid for appearances before tribunals. Women frequently cannot afford lawyers to represent them. If they haven't got backing from a union or other organisation they have to appear in person – perhaps facing a lawyer acting for the employer. This puts women at a great disadvantage. (The National Council for Civil Liberties and the Equal Opportunities Commission will back individual women taking cases.)

2. Women have to apply personally – the union cannot apply for them. Nor can groups of women get together and apply as a class or group. Each case must be treated separately. This puts great pressure on applicants. In the United States, an individual or a small number of people can apply to the court on behalf of a whole group or 'class' of people. If the case is won then all others in the same position will benefit.

3. The process may be a great ordeal for a woman. She has to face the strain of court appearances; possibly the hostility and distrust of her workmates; and perhaps the vindictiveness of her employer.

4. It may be very difficult for a woman to obtain the necessary information on pay scales etc., particularly if she is acting alone and does not belong to a union. The employer, of course, has far better access to information.

5. The burden of proof is on the woman, i.e. she has to prove that she is being discriminated against, but the employer does not have to prove that he has *not* discriminated against her. This means that if the tribunal is unsure which side is right, it is the employer not the woman who is given the benefit of the doubt.

Sometimes equal pay can only be won by collective action. Brittain's Toy Factory Strike

MAGGIE MURRAY/FORMAT

COMPARING Jobs

HOW JOB EVALUATION STUDIES WORK

The basic rate of pay for a job usually depends on where it falls in the workplace grading scheme. Grading schemes come in an infinite variety of forms.

Grading schemes may be no more than an *ad hoc* **structure – determined largely by what the employer decides you will be paid on the day you start work. But in larger workplaces, particularly where there is efficient union organisation, there is usually some agreed structure and people are graded according to established rules.**

WHAT DOES DOES JOB EVALUATION MEAN?

Job evaluation is just a system of rules for grading jobs: a formal procedure for comparing jobs so that their 'relative' value can be decided upon.

The point about job evaluation, however, is that it grades the *job*, by analysing the factors involved in it, not the *person* doing the job. Because of this it is often held up as being a 'scientifically neutral' procedure for valuing jobs. Employers usually claim that it is objective and unbiased.

There are many different types of schemes. Most of them operate by choosing factors which are considered important – such as effort, responsibility, working conditions, skills etc. The more of the elements found in a particular job, the more 'valuable' the job and therefore the higher it will be graded.

HOW IT'S DONE: SOME METHODS OF JOB EVALUATION

*Ranking

This is one of the simpler methods. Jobs are placed in order of importance, ranked individually and then grouped into grades. The way in which the 'importance' of a job is decided varies. It might be done on the basis of job titles. More likely, however, is that a job description will be drawn up for each job, and certain factors will then determine where the job goes in the ladder.

*Paired Comparisons

With this method, key jobs are selected – say five key jobs. Each of these key jobs is then compared with each other and given a score according to whether it is thought to be worth more, the same or less than the other job. When each of the five jobs has been compared, the scores are added up thus giving each of them a score or 'value' – and they are rated accordingly.

These five jobs then serve as a *benchmark*. Other jobs not included in the first exercise are then slotted in according to how they are felt to compare to the key jobs.

This system is sometimes referred to as the 'felt fair' system. The jobs are in effect graded according to what is 'felt fair'.

*Points Rating

This is the type of system which is most associated with job evaluation, although it comes in many different forms. The basics of it are as follows:

i. You have to decide on what factors in the job determine the degree of difficulty or responsibility of the job – i.e. what factors add 'value' to the job. The number of factors and the type of factors chosen will vary depending on the scheme. Some schemes may include only half a dozen or so, others may involve 30 or 40 or more different factors. For example, a scheme for manual workers might include physical effort, manual skill, monotony, responsibility etc.

ii. Once the factors have been chosen, each is given a range of points. For example, manual dexterity might be given a range of 10 – 20 points. A job which demands only a small amount of manual dexterity might therefore rate 10 points for this factor, whereas one involving a lot of manual dexterity could score 20 points.

iii. Once this has been done for each factor, and applied to each job, the jobs are then ranked according to the total number of points they have acquired. Ultimately, those jobs with the greater number of points should be paid more. This method forces the analyst to say whether, for example, physical strength is given a higher range of points than manual dexterity. If physical strength is more valued than manual dexterity women will do less well than men in the final score.

IS IT AN OBJECTIVE SYSTEM?

If you look carefully at the sort of job evaluation schemes outlined above you will see that there are plenty of ways in which prejudice or bias could creep into a scheme. Here are a few of them:

* *All the schemes involve subjective decisions. Rating jobs involve someone deciding which job he or she thinks is 'worth' the most. This is particularly true of the paired comparison scheme. Even with the points rating scheme it has to be decided how important a particular factor is in a job and how many points it should score.*

* *Most schemes involve the drawing up of a job description. How a job is described can vary enormously depending on who is describing it. For example, the person doing the job may take part of a job for granted and therefore omit to mention it – such as a receptionist who may in practice regularly deal with customers' enquiries over the phone when the boss is not there – but not really see it as part of her job. On the other hand, an outsider drawing up a job descrip-*

tion may not be aware of some of the skills involved because s/he has set ideas about what skills are needed. For example, someone drawing up a job description for a canteen assistant may see only menial, fairly dirty jobs, with little responsibility involved. In fact, there may well be an element of responsibility – if, for example, powerful chemicals are used for cleaning and these have to be stored and used with care.

* Most schemes involve the choosing of relevant factors which will count in deciding how valuable your job is. If some of the factors in your job are not included in the chosen list, you can't score a value for them. So this is an area where there can be a great deal of bias. For example, a scheme may award some points for having to work in unpleasant physical conditions. Thus, workers who have to go in and out of a storeroom in an outside yard might score some points since sometimes the weather is likely to be cold. But another job, say on an assembly line, might involve having to sit in one position doing a very repetitive motion with one arm. The physical conditions of the room may be warm and pleasant enough, but having to sit in one position and not being able to move about might be just as unpleasant as having to go out into a cold yard. But unless the people doing the job evaluation recognise this as a factor, the assembly workers would not be able to score anything.

Even if you've got all the factors you want counted in a scheme, someone has still got to decide whether they think your job includes that factor, and if so how important a part of your job they think it is and what sort of score within the possible range of points they think it should get.

In practice, unless a great deal of thought and preparation is put into a scheme it can be very biased – and can just reproduce existing values about what traditional women's work is worth.

IS IT WORTH BOTHERING?

Job evaluation can be a useful tool – provided you know what you're doing with it and you know what results you want at the end of it. But the development of a scheme and the evaluation of jobs is a complicated task and requires a great deal of bargaining and negotiating with employers. Employers after all, will know what they want out of the scheme before it is introduced. It is essential that unions are involved in negotiating the terms of reference of a job evaluation study if the exercise is to serve the interests of the employees.

A job evaluation scheme can be a way of dealing with anomalies, of forcing people to argue about the value of jobs and of forcing them to justify why certain jobs are low-graded. A job evaluation scheme can be one way of exposing the fact that the pay gradings are based on prejudice rather than on the real value of the jobs.

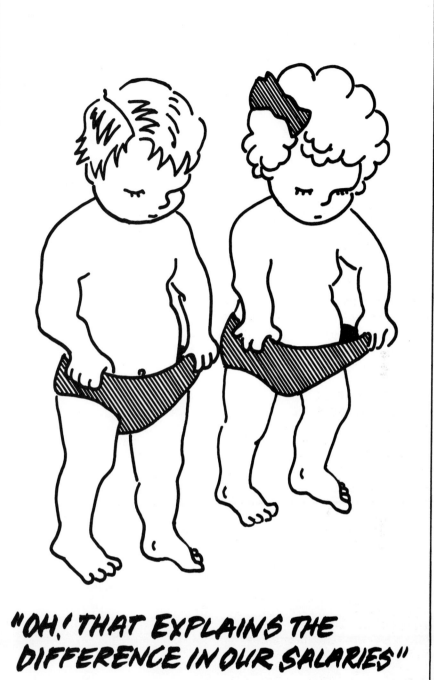

"OH! THAT EXPLAINS THE DIFFERENCE IN OUR SALARIES"

ANON

But if job evaluation is to be used effectively to up-grade women's jobs, then those taking part in it need to understand the system fully, to be properly trained (by their union and not just by management) and need to be able to have a full say in how jobs are evaluated.

DISCUSSION POINTS
Make a list of ways in which job evaluation schemes can involve bias. Try and think of specific examples of how this works out in practice.

If you are a member of a union, discuss the role the union should play in a job evaluation exercise.

THE NAME OF THE Game

The label of a job can often mask its content. Women doing more or less the same work as men are often given different job titles. For example:

MEN ARE:
Salesmen
Assistant Managers
Technicians
Office Managers
Personal Assistants

WOMEN ARE:
Shop Assistants
Manager's Assistants
Operators
Typing Supervisors
Secretaries

WHEREAS FOR ME THEY SAY IT IS THE NATURAL THING TO DO— IT'S WHAT I'M EXPECTED TO BE GOOD AT. THEREFORE I GET PAID LESS FOR IT. LUCKY ME!

FOR ME THIS IS REAL WORK.

PRACTICAL EXERCISE

The following exercise is based on a case which was heard by an industrial tribunal in Manchester. Using the information we give you, can you decide – on the basis of our present legislation – whether the industrial tribunal should award the women equal pay or not? Then compare your arguments to the tribunal's decision which you will find over the page.

THE PROBLEM

Mrs McCabe, with seven other women, worked as a machine shop operator for a well known computer firm. Before the Equal Pay Act the men were also called machine shop operators but were paid more.

When the Act came into force in 1975 the women claimed and received equal pay with their male colleagues. But shortly after this there was a job evaluation study and the men were upgraded to become 'fabrication assemblers' and were paid more than the women. The company claimed this was so as to pay them the same as men doing similar work at another factory. It was intended that the men would have some training and so be more flexible in their work.

Only two men had training and in practice the men's work remained largely the same as the women's. Here is how the two jobs look:

FABRICATION ASSEMBLERS	MACHINE SHOP OPERATORS
Men	Women
Heavier work	Lighter work
Set their own drills	Able to set their own drills but not allowed to
Flexibility in job description	Less flexibility
Less dexterity	Greater dexterity
Training available but only 2 men had taken the opportunity	Training not available

(Remember, some of the differences would have been there when the women got equal pay in 1975.)

CHRISTINE ROCHE

HYGIENE operative

CLEANER

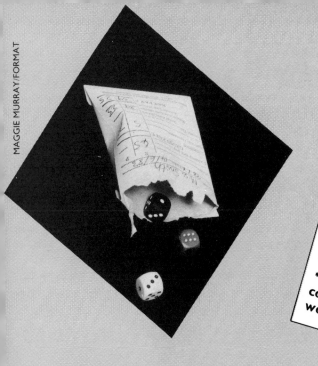

Should The Women Be Paid The Same As The Men?

Do you think the industrial tribunal should give the women equal pay?

Here are some questions you may like to discuss.

* How had the men's jobs changed when they were 'up-graded'?

* What do you think 'flexibility' in the men's jobs means?

* Do you think the employers were trying to comply with the spirit of the Equal Pay Act? If not, in what way were they trying to evade their responsibilities?

* If you were going to conduct a job evaluation study in the computer firm, how would you evaluate the men's and the women's jobs?

Decision of Industrial Tribunal

The IT held that the women's work and the men's work was of a broadly similar nature. Although there were some differences, these were based in the main on physical attributes and therefore on the sex of the operator. For example, the men did heavy work and the women lighter work – but this was counter-balanced by the dexterity of the women. Also the men set their own drills, but the women were not allowed to do so, although some of them were capable of it. These were not differences of practical importance. The tribunal noted that many of these jobs had been divided between the men and the women in the same way when the respondent company had agreed that the women were entitled to equal pay in 1975. With regard to the job evaluation scheme, although the scheme was a valid and genuine evalution study, the men were not genuinely placed in higher grade jobs and any pay variation was not justified. The men were not flexible in any real sense. The tribunal also held that there was insufficient flexibility in the men's work to constitute a material difference. This so-called flexibility had existed prior to 1975 and thereafter there was no substantial change in the work the men and women did, which was broadly similar. Even the two men with training were treated the same as the others. The IT awarded the women equal pay.

CHRISTINE ROCHE

How can we get equal pay for work of equal value?

WHAT NCCL WANTS

NCCL believes that equal pay for work of equal value should be incorporated into our equal pay legislation and used with the least amount of bureaucracy possible. When tribunals and the Central Arbitration Committee hear 'equal value' cases, they should have a common sense approach using the criteria of a non-discriminatory job evaluation scheme without the formality of a job evaluation scheme. Equality officers would investigate a woman's claim and report to the industrial tribunal.

WHAT OTHER COUNTRIES DO

REPUBLIC OF IRELAND

In the Irish Republic, where the equal value clause is part of the Anti-Discrimination (Pay) Act 1974, a woman can claim equal pay with a man whose work and working conditions are different from hers. Nor is it necessary to go through a job evaluation exercise, as the claimant is entitled to draw up the job description in any way she likes and make an argument based on those descriptions. The Irish model is a good example of how an equal value clause is used effectively and without undue formality. The following examples show how the 'felt fair' approach is used in Ireland. The

Equality Officer investigates an equal value claim, weighs up the different elements of the jobs and then arrives at a conclusion which 'feels fair'. There is no attempt to award points, unlike many quasi-scientific job evaluation studies.

Examples

1. THE TRALEE CHAINSAW CASE

Borg-Warner (Ireland) Limited and Irish Transport and General Workers Union

In 1981, 128 women claimed that their jobs were equal in value to the work done by the utility maintenance person (a man). The women's jobs were assembly operatives, repairers, parts salvagers, assembly demonstrator/trainers, spare parts storekeepers and a canteen operative. The women earned between

£69.22 and £74.60 per week. The male utility maintenance person earned £79.39 per week.

The union and company agreed job descriptions for each of the jobs with the Equality Officer. The union and company then submitted their own assessment of each job. The Equality Officer then visited the factory and interviewed the workers.

The Equality Officer looked at the demands of each of the women's jobs and gave a recommendation on whether *overall* they were less demanding or of equal value to the utility maintenance person. The Equality Officer found that the work of the operatives was not equal in value because they only had to perform one operation at a time, the work appeared to require less ability and physical effort and overall the working conditions of the operators appeared to be less demanding than that of the utility maintenance person. The Equality Officer gave similar sorts of reasons for not recommending equal pay for work of equal value for the other women *except* the material handlers and the demonstrator/trainers.

The Equality Officer found that the knowledge and skill required of the demonstrator/trainers was greater than that required by the utility maintenance person. While his job required more physical effort and the working conditions were less pleasant, the Equality Officer considered that this was balanced by the considerable responsibility involved in training and monitoring the performance of new assembly operators.

The Equality Officer thought that the work of the material handlers required as much skill and greater mental effort than the work of the utility maintenance person.

It was recommended that the women doing these two jobs should be awarded equal pay.

2. THE CASE OF THE BREAST MAKERS
Medeering Limited and Irish Transport and General Workers Union

In 1977, the Irish Transport and General Workers Union (ITGWU) represented 20 female assemblers who worked for Medeering Limited making breast prostheses (false breasts for women who have had surgery). The union claimed that the work performed by the women (who did various tasks) was equal in value to the work of the male moulders.

The men's work was fairly heavy (over a prolonged period) and they were on their feet all the time in hot noisy conditions. They had a certain amount of responsibility for the quality of the product in that they had to use the correct amount of plastisol and see that oven temperatures were right and that plugs and mould were completely free of dust.

The women did various jobs on the assembly line – inspection, sanding, form-shaping, cementing, filling, extracting all bubbles with a 'gun', stamping, packing and despatch.

The union argued that all the women were required to be flexible and to do jobs on the line other than their own. The main points of the union's case were:

(i) The women were responsible for all but the first stage in the process – they actually made the final product. As the product was assembled they were responsible for not damaging it and catching any faults that might develop. The effect of a flaw could be serious.

(ii) Training was carried out by fellow workers. All the women had responsibility for the 3 week training period for newcomers.

(iii) The men's work was unskilled but was performed in far less pleasant working conditions than the women's work and also required more physical effort. To balance this, the women's work was semi-skilled and required great flexibility and heavy responsibility for the end product.

The Equality Officer was called into the factory and evaluated the work of the moulders and the tasks involved in assembling and filling the plastic moulds.

The Equality Officer then made a recommendation to the Labour Court. Overall the Equality Officer found that the work performed by the female assemblers – especially the digital dexterity required – was as demanding as the physical energy expended by the moulders in the performance of their work.

The Equality Officer recommended that the female assemblers were entitled to equal pay with the male moulders. Although the ruling was never implemented, it is a good example of how equal value may be assessed.

UNITED STATES

In the USA over the last ten years there has been a great increase in job evaluation in the public service sector at both Federal and State level. This is partly the result of unions pressing for comparability with the better-paid private sector (as in the UK). Job evaluation studies have made women more aware of the extent to which they are underpaid and undervalued and have provided the incentive to claim equal pay either by negotiation (sometimes resulting in strikes), or by action in the courts. The Equal Employment Opportunities Commission (similar to our Equal Opportunities Commission) is playing a vital role in pushing the concept of comparable worth (the same as our equal value) and many cases are settled before they get to court.

The American legal system allows for the judgment of one case to settle for a whole group of people. This is called a 'class action' and is a reason why legal action in the United States on work of equal value can affect a very large number of women, not just the woman who brought the case.

Examples
1. THE CLERK AND THE VAN DRIVER
In Minnesota a job evaluation study of all state employees was undertaken by the State Council on the Economic Status of Women. It found that four female jobs – clerk typist, clerk, pharmacy technician and employment services assistant – had the same value as auto service senior mechanic and delivery van driver, both better-paid male jobs. The survey was instrumental in getting the new Minnesota Act which will give equal pay for work of equal value to all state employees. In both Minnesota and California, the State is required to examine female-dominated jobs (defined as containing 70% women) and carry out an evaluation of them.

2. THE BINDER AND THE CUTTER
In the case of *Thompson v Government Printing Office,* the US District Court held that Ms Thompson was entitled to equal pay for work of equal value under the Civil Service Reform Act 1978. Three hundred women employees who operated the large sewing machines in the bindery were entitled to the same pay as the men who operated the cutting and gathering machines. The men were called journeymen bookbinders, earning $11.94 per hour. The women, bindery workers, earned $8.11 per hour.

3. PRISON OFFICERS
The Supreme Court case of *Gunther v County of Washington* 1981 involved female guards at a local women's prison. A job evaluation study had rated their work as worth 95% of male prison guards' work. The men dealt with ten times as many prisoners per guard and the women did more 'lower value' administrative and clerical work. The court said that although they couldn't claim equal pay under the Equal Pay Act, because they weren't doing the same work as the men, the failure to raise their pay from 70% of the male rate to the 95% level found by the study was sex discrimination under the Civil Rights Act 1964 (the equivalent of our Sex Discrimination Act).

4. UNDERPAID AND UNDERVALUED
In San Jose, California, municipal employees went on strike in 1981 demanding comparable worth pay and an end to sex discrimination. The 2,000 workers, male and female (including clerks, janitors, librarians), were the first group of workers in the USA to strike over these demands. After a 10 day strike the employers agreed to reclassify the female-dominated jobs which had been 'underpaid' and 'undervalued'. About 700 workers have benefited from the agreement.

5. SEX DISCRIMINATION?

In Michigan the State Employees Association has brought a case alleging sex discrimination in pay. The case is still being heard. Two jobs cited in evidence are:

Secretary. 99.5% female workforce. Paid $12,882–$16,432 p.a.

Maintenance Mechanic. 100% male workforce. Paid $15,868–$19,961 p.a.

CANADA:
Equal Value is a Human Right

In Canada the concept of equal pay for work of equal value is contained in the Human Rights Act. The Canadian Human Rights Commission has the job of evaluating and comparing jobs falling under federal jurisdiction if requested to do so. A *complainant* must identify the group whose work she wishes to be compared with. Her work must be mainly performed by women and the other group's work must be mainly performed by men; and both groups must work in the same establishment.

Examples
1. Nurses and Hospital Technicians
Under the equal value clause nurses working in the Canadian federal prison were awarded the same pay as hospital technicians.

2. Librarians and Researchers
Government librarians were awarded equal pay with the higher paid, male dominated historical researchers. But librarians who did not work in the same workplace as the researchers had to get equal pay through collective bargaining as the Human Rights Act (like our Equal Pay Act) only allows comparisons in the same workplace.

3. Nurses or Physician's Assistants?
Public health nurses, who were paid $500 per month less than male physician assistants, who did similar work, claimed and won equal pay for work of equal value.

THE NETHERLANDS:
Finding a Comparable Man

A law of 1975 allows a woman to compare her wage to that commonly paid by the employer to a male employee performing work of equal value. If no such comparable man is employed, the woman may attempt to find a comparable man in a similar company. Where no job evaluation scheme exists, the job's value will be determined by the Equal Pay Commission.

Carshalton NHS Laundry

MAGGIE MURRAY/FORMAT

NCCL's Proposals

* NCCL believes that the Equal Pay Act should be properly amended to allow a woman to claim equal pay where she is employed on work which, in terms of the demands made on her, is of equal value to that of a man in the same employment. The demands may include physical or mental effort, accuracy, skill, training, responsibility for equipment or people, working conditions, stress and decision-making. The new Government regulations on equal value are totally inadequate.

* Equality Officers should be appointed in the UK who are trained and employed by the EOC to assist and report to industrial tribunals in equal value cases.

* A Code of Practice should be published by the Equal Opportunities Commission which will offer guidelines to industrial tribunals, the Central Arbitration Committee and the Equality Officers.

* All employees should receive an additional statement regarding the provisions of the revised Equal Pay Act with their terms and conditions of employment.

* Women who win equal value cases should be entitled to back pay up to 1975 (date of EEC Equal Pay Directive).

* Costs should not be awarded against the applicant unless the case is considered to have been 'frivolous'.

* Applicants to industrial tribunals should be able to bring *class actions*. A class action is a legal device, used effectively in the United States but unknown in this country, whereby a case can be taken on behalf of thousands of 'existing, future and potential' employees that are in the same group or 'class'. It enables individuals to seek a collective remedy and it enables a tribunal or court to make a binding decision regarding the whole group or 'class' affected by the dispute.

EQUAL PAY
FOR WORK OF EQUAL VALUE
YOUR RIGHTS UNDER THE NEW REGULATIONS

The Government has proposed new regulations amending the Equal Pay Act which will come into effect in 1984. These will allow a woman doing a different job from that of a man to claim that her work is equal in value to his. A woman doing work of equal value to a man (in terms of the demands made on her under headings such as effort, skill, and decisions) is now entitled to equal pay. A woman can only make an equal value claim if the man she is comparing herself with works for the same employer.

The new regulations have many shortcomings – the procedure is complex, lengthy and costly. The Government has also introduced the concept of the material factor, which means that employers will be able to argue that market forces (eg skill shortage, competition etc) justify paying men higher rates than women who are doing work of equal value. But there *is* the potential for women to challenge pay structures, including discriminatory job evaluation schemes. In theory the regulations will extend the scope of the Equal Pay Act to include many women who were not previously covered by the Act. By taking equal value claims women will be able to ask the industrial tribunal to reassess 'women's work', which has been traditionally undervalued in relation to men's work.

The Government reluctantly brought in the new regulations as a result of a ruling by the European Court of Justice in 1982. While our Equal Pay legislation now includes the right to equal pay for work of equal value, the Government has created a series of legal hurdles for women who decide to take an equal value claim to the industrial tribunal.

The complexity of the law makes it particularly important that you get legal advice if you want to make an equal value claim.

Who to approach if you want to claim equal pay for work of equal value:

1. If you are a member of a union, see your branch secretary or women's committee. Many unions can give you detailed legal advice and may be able to help you prepare your case and represent you at the tribunal hearing.
2. If you are not a member of a union, you could contact either the Rights for Women Unit, National Council for Civil Liberties or the Equal Opportunities Commission.

The law on equal pay for work of equal value will only be firmly established as a result of cases taken through the courts. If a woman loses her case under British law it is possible for her to take her case, on appeal, to the European Court. In the past few years the European Court has proved to be more progressive than British courts and many British women have benefitted as a result of appeals taken to the European Court of Justice.

WHAT ARE THEY WORTH?

SOME COMPARISONS OF MEN'S AND WOMEN'S WORK

FAIR DEAL?

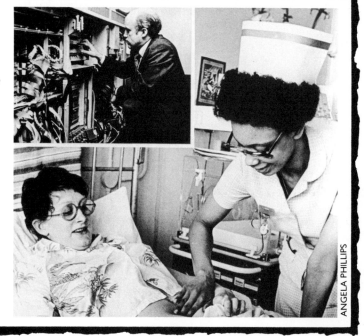

ANGELA PHILLIPS

Computer Engineer

Start:	HNC in Electronic Engineering at 18
Training:	Six months with extra 'new product' training + 3 – 7 years experience to become a systems engineer.
Hours:	37 per week mixed shifts with overtime. £12,000 per annum.

Nurse/Midwife

Start:	Three O levels at 18
Training:	Three years to Staff level + 2—3 years experience and specialist training to become a Charge Nurse.
Hours:	37½ per week mixed shifts
Pay:	with overtime. £6-7,000 per annum.

COMPARING A NURSERY NURSE WITH A CAR MECHANIC

School Leavers

Kevin and Valerie are both leaving school this year. Kevin wants to be a motor mechanic while Valerie would like to get a National Nursery Examination Board qualification and work with small children. Both have good school records and have been accepted as trainee employees by the local council.

Look particularly at their qualifications when they leave school and how much they earn at the beginning and end of their training.

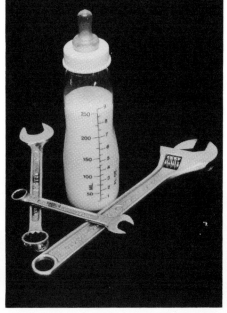

MAGGIE MURRAY/FORMAT

VALERIE	KEVIN
Age: 16	Age: 16
Qualifications:	Qualifications
G.C.E. 'O'-Levels	*C.S.E.*
English Language, English Literature, History, Domestic Science, Maths (C.S.E. Grade 1)	Technical Drawing, Mathematics English, Science

VALERIE: Nursery Nurse

Valerie is one of just 12 (from over 600 applicants) who will train as a nursery nurse while being employed by the local authority. Most girls and boys doing their NNEB have to go to college for two years on a grant. Valerie will spend 60% of her time at college and 40% in various nurseries.

Although the course is intended to be practical, there is quite a lot of academic work to complete. The emphasis of the course will be the growth and development of the child from 0-7 years. Valerie will also have the opportunity to study for 'O'-level psychology or sociology. She will have to complete two written papers at the end of the course as well as complete a file of written child observations during practical work.

Qualified nursery nurses can work in either the education or social services sectors. Because she has been trained by a London local authority Valerie will probably work in a day nursery or nursery centre. She would be looking after under-fives during the day, usually while the mother and father are at work or because they are unable to look after the child. Together with health visiting and social work services, nursery staff keep in touch with parents who come to the nursery, giving help where necessary.

Valerie could specialise in looking after handicapped children or become a group leader for which she would get in-service training and an extra allowance. However, there is no career pattern for nursery nurses and unless she goes back to college to get a social work qualification, Valerie is unlikely to be appointed to a more senior position in her day nursery.

KEVIN: Car Mechanic

During his four-year apprenticeship, Kevin will go on block-release to his local technical college where he will prepare for his City and Guilds. He will spend a lot of his first year at college, learning about the detailed technology of the motor vehicle. Later he will concentrate on particular subjects like 'Diagnostic Techniques' or 'Compressed Air Braking Systems' and will have to take an examination in at least three of the subjects offered.

During the first few months in the garage, he will be involved in very general tasks and work alongside an experienced mechanic. Kevin will then be trained as a light motor mechanic – to test vehicles, recognise defects and carry out the necessary service and repair work. If Kevin shows promise and ambition he might be able to take the Advanced Craft certificate after his apprenticeship and then go on to further broadening studies such as junior management and super-

visory studies. If Kevin sits for the Licentiateship of the Institute (LCG) he will be recognised as a Master Craftsman.

Kevin knows that many supervisors started out on the shop floor and it is not unusual to find reception engineers and service managers in commercial garages still under 30.

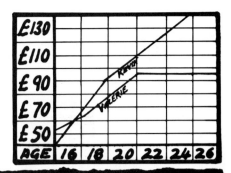

VALERIE'S EARNINGS

Age 16, on entry	£54.43 p.w. (£2,844 p.a.)
Age 18, qualified NNEB	£66.24 p.w. (£3,444 p.a.)
By the time she is 21	£93.93 p.w. (£4,884 p.a.)

As a nursery nurse, Valerie would be unlikely to earn much more than £5,000 (at present rates) whether she worked in a school, hospital, day centre or college creche. Unless she takes further qualifications she is likely to remain a nursery assistant or nursery officer on the same grade indefinitely.

KEVIN'S EARNINGS

Age 16, on entry	£50.41 p.w.
Age 17	£64.16 p.w. (+ bonuses)
Age 18	£82.49 p.w. (+ bonuses)
Age 19	£87.07 p.w. (+ bonuses)
	(bonuses will probably be around £20 p.w.)
Qualified Craftsman (at 19/20 years old)	£107.54 p.w. + £20-£45 bonus p.w.

If Kevin is promoted to being a chargehand he will earn an extra supplement. If he is successful and ambitious and has some in-service training, Kevin could become a foreman when he is about 27 or 28. He would then go on a different salary scale and earn £6,759-£7,479 p.a. (including London weighting) (£129.98-£143.82 per week) (1983 figures).

Kevin and Valerie leave school with fairly similar qualifications (although Valerie's 'O'-Levels will tend to be seen as having more value than Kevin's C.S.Es) and start similar courses with the same employer. Valerie needed higher entry qualifications but Kevin's apprenticeship is longer than Valerie's course.

Discussion points

1. The graph shows Valerie and Kevin's earnings. Discuss the pattern of earnings for each of them and then compare them. Do you think Kevin and Valerie have typical male and female earning patterns?

2. Does one job need more expertise than another? Do you think that it makes a difference if a person is looking after other people or a machine?

3. Using the information given, what job do you think Kevin and Valerie will be doing in 10 years' time? (Kevin is married with one child and Valerie lives with her boyfriend and has no children of her own.) Who will be paid most, who will have the better position, who will have most responsibility? Think of reasons to justify your answers.

COMPARING A SCHOOL COOK WITH A REFUSE COLLECTOR

Frieda: School Cook

Frieda is a school cook at a school with 1,000 pupils. She used to be a general assistant and then began cooking.

She was well suited to the work – she kept a cool head, could do several tasks at once and didn't flap when serving-up time was approaching. The supervisor suggested she went on day release classes and took her City and Guilds. She has now passed her exams and has just been appointed school cook.

As a school cook she is responsible to the cook-in-charge for the preparation and cooking of around 800 meals a day. A day's meal usually consists of a main meat dish and some salads, which are prepared and cooked on the premises. Each day she prepares fresh vegetables for cooking and mashes the potatoes. The sweet is usually a cake or bun – these need to be baked early in the morning and then iced or filled.

Although the cook-in-charge is responsible for re-ordering, Frieda is expected to notice any ingredients needing replacement. She assists with the serving of meals and then she and other kitchen staff have to clear and clean the kitchen ready for the next day.

A job evaluation to establish national grading of local authority workers has put school cooks on Grade F. Frieda works full-time for an average 36 hours, and earns £73.08 per week.

BERT: Refuse Collector

Bert is a refuse collector (dustman). He is 25 and has done various manual jobs on building sites, eventually managing to get a job with the local authority refuse collection department. He did not need any qualifications but had an interview with the supervisor.

As a refuse collector, Bert works in a gang of six men. He is collected at 7.30 a.m. from the local depot by the dust-bin lorry and the gang will empty approximately 1,000 bins during the day.

He is responsible for emptying the bin, putting it back tidily and closing the gate.

If the gang is not emptying bins outside houses, it may be removing the large refuse containers from the big estates or, occasionally, taking rubbish out of empty council-owned properties.

Bert is on Grade E (one grade lower than Frieda) of the pay structure. He works a 39 hour week and an average 2¼ hours overtime a week. He earns £110.80 per week.

Although dustmen's basic hourly pay is less than that of a school cook, their total hourly earnings are much higher because of bonus schemes (productivity payments). In spite of being a grade lower than the school cook, the dustman's weekly wage is £37.72 more than her weekly wage.

BREAKDOWN OF PAY FOR A DUSTMAN (Grade E) AND A COOK (Grade F)

	Basic Hourly Pay (Excl. Overtime)	Basic Hourly Pay (Incl. Overtime)	Unsocial Hours Payments	Product-ivity Pay-ments	Other	Total Hourly Earnings (Incl. Overtime)	Average Weekly Earnings	
	£	£	£	£	£	£	£	
Dustman Grade E	1.80	1.83	insignifi-cant	0.76	0.08	2.67	110.80	Dustman Grade E
Cook Grade F	1.86	1.86	0.03	0.05	0.09	2.03	73.08	Cook Grade F

(May 1982)

MAGGIE MURRAY/FORMAT

You can see from this example that agreements for *equal basic pay rates* **do not necessarily mean that there is** *equality of earnings*. **This is true of manual workers where there are usually several elements, besides the basic hourly rate, which make up the pay packet (e.g. productivity payments, overtime). You can also see from this example that you cannot simply compare male/ female hourly rates because men tend to work longer hours and be in jobs where they work more over-time – and therefore have a higher weekly wage than women.**

The main reason why dustmen take home £37 per week more than the cooks, who are on a higher grade, is because they have negotiated local productivity agreements (a bonus). The dustmen's productivity payments increase their hourly basic rate by *nearly half* as much again.

Many of these local schemes were introduced in the late 1960s and early 1970s, a time when the dustmen were particularly militant. During the local authority manual worker strikes in 1969 and 1970 dustmen were very much to the fore. However, employers refused to introduce a national bonus scheme for school meals staff in 1972 because the work study showed that school meals staff were already working at such high productivity levels that a productivity agreement would not increase output. No financial savings could be made to the service by introducing a bonus scheme, which needs to be self-financing.

QUESTIONS
When we talk about equal pay for jobs which are the same or are worth the same, do you think we should be talking about equal hourly rates or equal take home pay?

What are the reasons for women working shorter hours and less overtime?

Discussion points
Why have refuse collectors managed to negotiate productivity agreements while the school cooks have not?

What can you learn from these examples about ways in which men and women organise themselves at work?

Why do you think dustmen are more militant than school meals staff? Are there any particular reasons why it is difficult for school meals staff to organise themselves at work (e.g. only a few staff in each workplace, dealing with children)?

Different groups of people have different perspectives on the meaning of 'value'. Discuss what 'value' means to

> **a) employers**
> **b) consumers**
> **c) workers**

Can their different views of 'value' be reconciled?

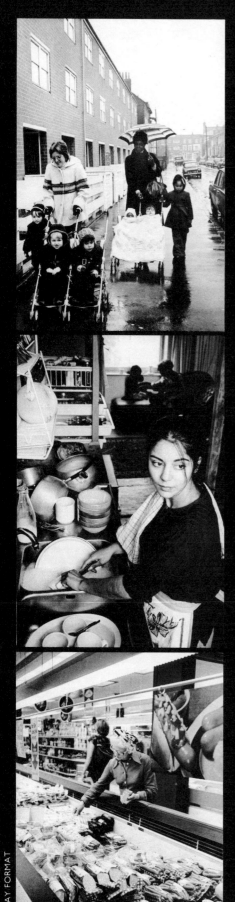

Position Vacant: HOUSEWIFE

Applications are invited for the position of manager of a lively team of four demanding individuals of differing needs and personalities. The successful applicant will be required to perform and co-ordinate the following functions: companion, counsellor, financial manager, buying officer, teacher, nurse, chef, nutritionist, decorator, cleaner, driver, child care supervisor, social secretary and recreation officer.

Qualifications: Applicants must have unlimited drive and the strongest sense of responsibility if they are to succeed in this job. They must be independent and self-motivated and be able to work in isolation and without supervision. They must be skilled in the management of people of all ages. They must be able to work under stress, for long periods of time if necessary. They must have flexibility to perform a number of conflicting tasks at one time without tiring. They must have the adaptability to handle all new developments in the life of the team, including emergencies and serious crises. They must be able to communicate on a range of issues with peoples of all ages, including public servants, school teachers, doctors, dentists, tradespeople, businesspeople, teenagers and children. They must be competent in the practical skills listed above. They must be healthy, creative, active and outgoing to encourage the physical and social development of the team members. They must have imagination, sensitivity, warmth, love and understanding, since they are responsible for the mental and emotional well-being of the team.

Hours of work: All waking hours and a 24-hour shift when necessary.

Pay: No salary or wage. Allowances by arrangement from time to time with the income-earning member of the team. The successful applicant may be required to hold a second job in addition to the one advertised here.

Benefits: No guaranteed holidays. No guaranteed sick leave, maternity leave or long service leave. No guaranteed life or accident insurance. No worker's compensation. No superannuation.

COMPARING A HOUSEWIFE WITH A MANAGING DIRECTOR

A woman with young children works at least 14 hours a day on a range of jobs as diverse as nursing and cost budgeting.

Using employment agencies' average fees for different jobs, Legal and General Insurance Company calculated that the commercial rate for a housewife's work is £279 per week, or £14,531 per year. This is equivalent to the salary of a sergeant major or certain grades of bishops, chief fire officer or head teacher.

Do you think these are fair comparisons?

In 1982, the pay levels for senior management in the top 34 UK companies ranged from £33,000-£150,000. The average salary (discounting fringe benefits) was £67,000. Typical earnings in smaller enterprises were:

Borough Treasurer of London Borough	£23,000
Group Finance Director in Midlands Engineering Company	£25,000 + car
Administration & Finance Manager in Lancashire Enterprises Ltd.	£11,000

POSITION VACANT:

MANAGING DIRECTOR OF SMALL FIRM

Applications are invited for the position of managing director of a small friendly company.

BASIC FUNCTION: Provides leadership, overall direction and administration of the operations of the Company. Interprets and applies the policies of the Board of Directors. Directs and generally supervises Company activities. Delegates portions of his responsibilities and authority when necessary, but may not delegate overall responsibility for results nor any portion of his accountability. Establishes a budget of operations and ensures that budget goal is achieved and cost objectives are met. Maintains close personal relationship with offices of important customers, prospective customers and vendors. Promotes satisfactory relations with industry and trade groups, press and public.

HOURS OF WORK: Applicant must be prepared to work longer than normal office hours but generous holiday allowance to compensate. Applicant must also be available for overseas travel, be prepared to undertake the arduous tasks of meeting new customers in first class hotels and be able to eat at least two four-course meals a day.

PAY: This will reflect the applicant's experience but will be upwards of £20,000 p.a.

BENEFITS: Generous holidays. Life and accident insurance; private health insurance for applicant and family; superannuation scheme; relocation expenses where appropriate.

Discussion points

1. Compare Deborah's job with the job of the managing director ... What do you think are the main similarities and the main points of difference?

2. What are the particular skills needed for the managing director's job and Deborah's job? Do you think some skills should be more highly rewarded than others? If so, how do you decide?

3. Prepare an equal value claim (to be compared with the managing director) for Deborah, aged 26, who has three children. The eldest, Sean, is 6½ years and goes to the local primary school which is a 15 minute walk away. Winston, aged nearly 4 years, goes to a playgroup which is 10 minutes in the opposite direction. He goes three mornings a week from 9.30-12 noon. Marlene is nearly a year old and is beginning to walk. She still has a sleep in the day and she needs a fresh food diet because she has a skin complaint. Ricky, Deborah's husband, is a bus driver and works alternating early and late shifts.

Draw up a timetable of Deborah's week and 'cost' it.

As a guide, use the following rates of pay: cleaner £2.50 per hour; cook/waitress/laundress £1.98 per hour; child-minder £1.84 per hour; nurse £2.40 per hour; supervisor £3.15 per hour; gardener £2.75 per hour; shopper/window cleaner £1.95 per hour.

100Kg.

POSITIVE Action

Positive Action is one way that women can be encouraged to do jobs which, in the past, have been done by men. Often the reason why women don't do particular jobs is because the employment *structure* is wrong, not because there is intentional discrimination against women.

Positive Action does *not* mean discrimination in reverse or preferring women to men. It means encouraging women to take up what opportunities there are and removing unnecessary hurdles to women's promotion. Unions can play an important part in identifying problems and bringing them into the ambit of negotiations.

NCCL has published a detailed guide to Positive Action but here are the main points of a Positive Action Programme. A Positive Action Programme will be most effective if it is negotiated between union and management. The union should be active at all stages of a Positive Action Programme.

HOW TO DO IT

A Programme for Positive Action At Work

1. An Equal Opportunity Employer

Commitment by an employer is important, especially if it is endorsed at top management level and well publicised (e.g. on all job advertisements). The Trades Union Congress has framed a model clause which can be incorporated into collective agreements.

2. Analyse the Workforce

Before there is a Positive Action Programme it is critical to have a full picture of the workforce. This will show up the categories and grades where there are no women. Areas of discrimination and disadvantage may be recognised for the first time. It is important that the union is fully involved in this often difficult exercise.

3. Examine Job Descriptions and Requirements

The next stage is to see whether jobs are described as though only a man or a woman could do it. It is necessary to examine all jobs to determine which requirements are essential and which merely discourage one sex from applying for the job. For instance, Belinda Price won a case in an industrial tribunal because she argued that the civil service age limit of 28 years for the executive grade of the civil service indirectly discriminated against women. Women who wanted to enter the civil service after looking after young children were less likely to be able to comply. Length of experience, minimum qualifications, height requirements, mobility requirements and shift working are all requirements which could be more difficult for a woman to meet than a man.

4. Recruiting and Advertising

A thorough examination of recruiting and advertising policy should be undertaken in order to ensure that women are encouraged to apply for all types of jobs. For example, a company could adopt a policy of advertising traditionally 'male' jobs in papers mainly read by women.

5. Application, Selection Tests and Interviews

Application forms should be scrutinised to make sure that they are not biased against women, for example by asking questions about domestic responsibilities or number of children. Employers could also make it clear to applicants that time spent out of the labour market looking after children will not be regarded as wasted and will be taken into account as useful experience.

It is particularly important to eliminate any conscious or unconscious bias against women in the interview procedure. An essential part of this will be training of the interviewing panel.

6. Promotion

As in hiring, promotion posts should be advertised throughout the workplace and not contain unnecessary qualifying provisions. It should be made clear that applications from women will be welcomed.

7. Training

Training opportunities should be as accessible to women as to men, in particular part-timers or women who cannot leave their families to take part in evening or residential courses. It is legal to set up special women-only training programmes if a particular job is done mainly or exclusively by men.

8. Children

As responsibility for childcare remains in the hands of women, employers should take account of this when they set out to encourage women to apply for jobs. Some things which the union should negotiate for are:

- Workplace creches
- Time off for parents with sick children (fathers as well as mothers)
- Flexible working hours
- Job-sharing

9. Written Agreement

When it has been decided which positive steps are most appropriate to the workplace in question, a written agreement should be drawn up in consultation with the union. It is important that all employees are made aware of the details of the agreement.

Positive Action In The Unions

Unions are an important link in negotiating positive action programmes with the employer. But women are also under-represented on union decision-making bodies. Some unions have adopted a Positive Action Programme to ensure that women are more fully represented. For example, the National Union of Public Employees has reserved five seats for women on its executive council. Many unions have special women's committees or equal opportunities committees to encourage a greater awareness of issues which affect women.

The Trades Union Congress has adopted a charter, *Equality For Women Within Trade Unions*, which sets out ten measures to encourage greater participation by women in union activities.

1. The National Executive Committee of the Union should publicly declare to all its members the commitment of the union to involving women members in the activities of the union at all levels.

2. The structure of the union should be examined to see whether it prevents women from reaching the decision-making bodies.

3. Where there is large membership of women but no women on the decision-making bodies special provision should be made to ensure that women's views are represented, either through the creation of additional seats or by co-option.

4. The National Executive Committee of each union should consider the desirability of setting up advisory committees within its constitutional machinery to ensure that the special interests of its women members are protected.

5. Similar committees at regional, divisional and district level could also assist by encouraging the active involvement of women in the general activities of the union.

6. Efforts should be made to include in collective agreements provision for time off without loss of pay to attend branch meetings during working hours where that is practicable.

7. Where it is not practicable to hold meetings during working hours, every effort should be made to provide childcare facilities for use by either parent.

South London Comprehensive School

8. Childcare facilities, for use by either parent, should be provided at all district, divisional and regional meetings and particularly at the union's annual conference and for training courses organised by the union.

9. Although it may be open to any members of either sex to go to union training courses, special encouragement should be given to women to attend.

10. The content of journals and other union publications should be presented in non-sexist terms.

Discussion points

1. Do you agree with the idea of Positive Action?

2. Examine your workplace under each of the headings of the Positive Action Programme. Would it benefit from a Positive Action policy?

3. If you are a member of a union, what measures would you like to see adopted at branch and/or national levels to encourage women to participate?

4. If you are a woman, make a list of all the reasons why you are not doing a more senior or better-paid job. Discuss within the group the extent to which your career has been determined by (i) circumstances (ii) choice.

MAGGIE MURRAY/FORMAT

And Now...

WHAT'S YOUR JOB WORTH?

Here is a guide for a do-it-yourself evaluation of *your* job. Like any 'job evaluation' exercise it is not scientific but it will give you some idea of what your job is worth. It will raise some of the issues involved in 'equal pay for work of equal value'.

(Please note: this sheet is written for a woman who wants to compare her job to a job being done by a man. If your group is mixed, the men should choose a woman's job and compare it with their own. Would they expect to be paid more than the woman gets if they did her job? If you are not working, take the job your mother/sister/friend does and compare it with a man's job.)

A DO-IT-YOURSELF EVALUATION

If you want to show that the job you do is of equal value to a different job done by a man you must make out a convincing case that *if a man did your job he would be paid more*. In other words, if you work in a job where there are no men at your workplace, you need to work out what would be the male rate for the job if the job were normally done by men not women.

Stage One

Find a man who is earning as much as you think you *should* be paid if you were a man doing your job. Look at his job and your job. In separate columns write down a list of the main tasks and responsibilities of the two jobs. Your list may look something like this:

Elsa is a home help and paid £70.20 for a 39 hour week and George is an assembly worker at Fords and is paid £119.91 for a 39 hour week (day shifts).

Next, points are awarded (out of 10) for each of the qualities listed below. Working conditions e.g. noise and dirt should also be taken into account. These are qualities usually applied in any simple job evaluation exercise. Remember, job evaluation studies are not scientific. The list may look something like this:-

Elsa		George
7	skill	8
9	physical effort	7
5	mental effort	7
9	responsibility	7
8	working conditions	9
38		**38**

You can see that, although George earns £49.71 per week more than Elsa, in our comparison their points balance out and you could argue that the jobs are of equal value.

Now fill in the sheet with details of your job and a man's job you want to compare it with. The points are used as an approximate estimate of the relative value of each quality for the man and the woman.

RESPONSIBILITIES AND TASKS

ELSA/HOME HELP	GEORGE/ASSEMBLY LINE WORKER
Responsible for clients	Responsible for machinery
Many operations – flexibility required	2 or 3 semi-skilled operations
Unsupervised working	Has to work in co-operation with others on line
Use of domestic machinery	Use of hand tools
Ability to use chemicals, detergents	Ability to understand instructions

MAGGIE MURRAY/FORMAT

I. PAY & CONDITIONS: fill in all the details you can

YOUR JOB		MAN'S JOB
	Pay (before tax)	
	Hours	
	Basic hourly rate (i.e. weekly pay divided by hours)	
	Bonus scheme (average per week)	
	Average overtime pay per week	
	Holiday allowance	
	Other benefits	

2. TASKS & RESPONSIBILITIES

YOUR JOB	Main characteristics of job	MAN'S JOB

3. NOW AWARD POINTS OUT OF TEN

YOUR JOB		MAN'S JOB
	skill	
	physical effort	
	mental effort	
	responsibility	
	working conditions	
	TOTAL	

Now compare the points you have awarded for each job. Are they more-or-less equivalent? If you find that the man's job has more points than your job, or that his higher earnings are as a result of longer hours, then lower your sights and repeat the exercise with a man earning less but still more than you.

If you want to pursue your claim you should contact your shop steward or the women's committee in your union and ask them to take your case up on your behalf. If you are not a member of a union you could contact NCCL Women's Rights Unit, 21 Tabard Street, London SE1 4LA or the Equal Opportunities Commission, Overseas House, Quay Street, Manchester M3 3HN.

Role Play

UNION AND MANAGEMENT NEGOTIATE ON EQUAL PAY FOR WORK OF EQUAL VALUE

WHAT YOU DO

This exercise will help you to formulate the arguments which can be used for and against claiming work of equal value. You should divide into two groups and act out the part of either union or management. Photocopy this page and cut as indicated so that the union group has only the information headed 'The Union'. It is important that the management representatives *feel* themselves to be arguing on behalf of the company and vice versa. Both groups should have copies of the job descriptions and background as this is information available to both sides.

The case study, which is based on the case from the Irish Labour Court described on page 15, may either be used as an exercise in direct negotiations between management and union, or in presenting a case before an industrial tribunal. After both sides have put their case, you may want to decide that only *some* of the women are doing jobs of equal value to the moulders.

BACKGROUND TO THE DISPUTE

The company is involved in the manufacture, to medical specifications, of breast prostheses. The union claims that the work done by female employees is equal in value in terms of skill, physical or mental effort, responsibility and working conditions, to that performed by the male employees. They are therefore entitled to equal pay. Management dispute the claim.

All the women are paid the same rate.

The job descriptions of the three moulders, who are men, and the eight assemblers, who are women, are listed below. The women are expected to be able to do more than one task during the day and all of them would be able to perform the tasks described in points (b)-(j) below.

JOB DESCRIPTIONS

THE MEN

Moulders: There are three men employed as moulders. They pour measured amounts of plastisol into moulds, replace and screw down the top of the moulds, fasten the moulds on rotational hubs in ovens for a few minutes to cure, before placing in the cooler at the end of the curing cycle. The moulds are taken from the cooler, unscrewed, each shell is removed and placed over a foam cradle in trays. The moulds are mostly 1-2 stone in weight, though there are some heavier ones. Each man lifts 12-16 moulds every eleven minutes.

The work is fairly heavy (over a prolonged period) and the men are on their feet all the time in hot noisy conditions. They have a certain amount of responsibility for the quality of the product in that they must use the correct amount of plastisol and see that oven temperatures are right and that plugs and moulds are completely free of dust.

THE WOMEN

a) Inspector: Two women are employed as inspectors. Each shell is stretched manually in order to find flaws. The inspector must be able to notice minute colour differences, holes, air bubbles, variations in thickness etc. The shells are weighed and are also tested with a liquid chemical to prove that they have been sufficiently cured (heated). Faulty items are discarded and if a batch is faulty the inspector stops the process in the moulding room. The inspector has to keep a record of her inspection on five different record sheets.

The job requires a very high level of visual concentration and considerable manual dexterity. If faults are not detected the shells could burst in wearing. Training takes about three months and it takes about a year to build up full speed. At standard production rate each inspector examines up to approximately 700-800 shells per day.

b) Sanding: This worker sands off any edges of PVC along the seam of each shell. She must be careful not to cut the shell with the sandpaper. She injects each item with glycol through a hole made in the shell during moulding. The purpose of this injection is to permit free movement of the shell during further manufacture. Care must be taken to insert the needle absolutely straight and not puncture the shell. The operator then puts all the items on trays, attaches tickets to the tray, recording the number of products processed, and loads them on shelves.

c) Form Shaping: This worker cuts different-sized forms (shapes) from oblong or square pieces of foam with an electrically heated wire. She replaces the wire after about eight shapes are cut. She places the pieces of foam on a template, which is revolved to allow the wire to cut through the foam. The speed of the revolving template and the heat of the wire are related. If either the heat or the speed is incorrect the foam will be damaged. The job requires a very steady hand, keeping the wire straight and steady.

Care must be taken to avoid burning and ensure the top and bottom of the shapes are the correct size. The plates have to be washed regularly with chemicals and changed for different sizes of product. The pieces of foam left after the shapes have been cut are retained for packing.

d) Cementing: This worker pastes one side of the shell, places the foam shape in the shell, absolutely straight, and compresses the two. Unless pressure is correctly applied the shell will wrinkle and the product will probably have to be rejected. She examines the edges of the foam and patches down any areas where the foam has not adhered properly to the shell. The job requires accuracy and concentration.

e) Filling: The worker stands in front of a trough from which needles project. She mounts each form (i.e. the shell and foam backing) on the needles and injects fluid. She must also regulate the amount of fluid to be injected into the product as there is a medically approved weight for the various sizes of product. She then weighs each form and adjusts each for over or underfilling. She must be careful not to puncture the shell by putting the form on the needle incorrectly. The average daily output is approximately 700-800.

f) De-Airing: This worker extracts air bubbles in the shell with a 'gun' with an extracting needle, checks the weight of the forms making any necessary adjustments to the liquid and cements the air hole. The job demands accuracy and care as the shell could be damaged by the needle in extracting the air and could afterwards leak during wearing.

g) Patching: This worker cleans shells which may have become slightly dirty in handling, using a chemical liquid to do so. She checks the edges of the shell and the foam back and if the cementing has come unstuck, patches any such edges down. She checks that forms have not got any flaws which might cause them to burst in handling or in wearing.

h) Stamping: This worker weighs each form and stamps its weight and size on the foam backing. She also stamps the weight and size on the covers for the form and shelves these covers. It is important that this information be correct as it is used as a reference if any alterations are needed later by a customer.

i) Packing: This worker puts covers on the completed forms, packs them together with a multi-language instruction sheet in small boxes and stamps the boxes with the weight and date.

j) Despatch: This worker stencils the destination on large boxes, numbers the boxes and packs the small boxes in the large boxes which are then weighed.

N.B. Each of the assembly line workers keeps a record of the number of products she has processed each day.

THE UNION

You have to prepare and put your claim to management that the women do work of equal value to the men and therefore should be paid at the same rate. The law is that equal pay should be paid for work of equal value. You should try and incorporate some of the ideas and arguments you have found in this book. These are additional arguments you might want to consider:

a) Though each woman has her 'own' job, she has at times to move to other jobs on the assembly line.

b) The women do all but the first stage in the process. As the product is assembled, each woman has a responsibility not to damage it and to catch faults that may develop or that may have been missed at an earlier stage. The effect of any flaw or leak would be very damaging for the wearer.

c) Most of the training is done by fellow workers. Training generally involves work on rejects for about three weeks under the supervision of a fellow worker. It takes at least three months to build up to full speed. All the women have a responsibility for training newcomers.

d) The men's work is unskilled, but is done in much worse conditions and also requires more physical effort. To balance this, the women's work is semi-skilled, requires great flexibility, considerable experience and a great deal of responsibility for the product.

THE COMPANY

You have to prepare your response to the Union's claim for equal pay for the eight women workers.

These are some of the arguments you may want to consider:

a) Employees are not discriminated against on the grounds of sex. They are paid according to the work they do. A female moulder (if one were to be employed) would be paid at the same rate as a male moulder.

b) Care, diligence, an eye for quality and pride in the standard of the work are common to all the jobs. Both the moulders and the assembly line workers have to be flexible in the tasks they perform in their own departments. Most people could do the assembly work after a short period of training. But the same is not true for the moulders because of the physical effort required in the moulding area.

c) The finished product depends on the quality of the moulding. If the moulding is bad, there are difficulties all along the line. In the assembly section, most faults that occur can be corrected as soon as they are discovered.

d) The moulding work cannot be classed as unskilled. There are seven operations involved, and each must be watched carefully to avoid making a reject.

e) The moulding operation must be performed in a relatively high temperature. It involves continuous lifting of heavy mould assemblies into and out of the machines.

f) The assembly operation is light work carried out generally in a sitting position in a nearly ideal atmosphere. The two operations can't therefore be considered to be of equal value because of the differences in physical effort and working conditions.

RESOURCE LIST
ORGANISATIONS

National Council for Civil Liberties
21 Tabard Street London SE1 4LA (01 403 3888)

Equal Opportunities Commission
Overseas House Quay Street Manchester M3 3HN (061 833 9244)

Trades Union Congress
Congress House 23/28 Great Russell Street London WC1 (01 636 4030)

Rights of Women
374 Grays Inn Road London WC1 (01 278 6349)

Part-Time Workers Campaign
21 Ensdon Grove Kingstanding Birmingham B44 0GH

Citizens Advice Bureau
(for general information and address of local bureau) 110 Drury Lane London WC2 (01 836 9231)

Law Centres Federation
(for address of local law centres) 164 North Gower Street London NW1 (01 387 8570)

FURTHER READING
NATIONAL COUNCIL FOR CIVIL LIBERTIES PUBLICATIONS (Please enclose 20p for postage for orders under £2, 35p for orders under £5 and 75p for larger orders)

WOMEN'S RIGHTS – THE PENGUIN GUIDE £3.95 Anna Coote and Tess Gill. The complete guide to women's rights, new revised edition. (Penguin 1981)

WOMEN'S RIGHTS £2.95 Marion Lowe. A series of information sheets and discussion notes covering Abortion, Education and Training, Equal Opportunities at Work, Equal Pay, Rape and Domestic Violence, Social Security, Taxation, Women, Work and Childcare. A4 Pack. (NCCL 1981)

TAKING LIBERTIES £3.95 Jean Coussins. Teaching pack containing 18 work cards, booklet and poster. An introduction to Equal Rights primarily for schools. (Virago 1979)

MATERNITY RIGHTS FOR WORKING WOMEN 95p Jean Coussins. Updated to cover the latest legislation, this practical guide explains how women can get maternity benefits and leave. Invaluable reading for any woman who wants to return to work after having a baby. (NCCL 1983)

PART-TIME WORKERS NEED FULL-TIME RIGHTS 95p Ann Sedley. All the rights of part-time workers, and how NCCL thinks the law should change. (NCCL 1980)

SEX DISCRIMINATION IN SCHOOLS 95p Harriet Harman. Looks at the extent of discrimination in schools and the legislation that is supposed to fight it. (NCCL 1978)

POSITIVE ACTION FOR WOMEN: THE NEXT STEP £2.00 Sadie Robarts with Anna Coote and Elizabeth Ball. This book draws on the experience of those in the USA and this country who have sought to implement equal opportunities and proposes model Positive Action programmes. (NCCL 1981)

SEXUAL HARASSMENT AT WORK 95p Ann Sedley and Melissa Benn. Sexual harassment is now recognised as a major problem facing women at work. This book looks at how common the problem is, how women are organising to oppose it and what trade unions can do. (NCCL 1982)

INCOME TAX AND SEX DISCRIMINATION 85p Patricia Hewitt. A practical guide to income tax, highlighting the injustices which still face women. (NCCL 1979)

SHIFT WORK SWINDLE 60p Jean Coussins. The arguments against the repeal of protective legislation for women in factories. (NCCL 1979)

AMENDING THE EQUALITY LAWS 95p Catherine Scorer and Ann Sedley. How the equality laws are failing and what should be done to make them effective. (NCCL 1983)

WOMEN AND WORK

WOMEN AT WORK £1.75 Chris Aldred. This book is concerned with trade union problems which confront women and discusses ways of dealing with the problems through changes at home at work and in the trade unions. (Pan Trade Union Studies 1981)

GETTING IT TOGETHER: WOMEN AS TRADE UNIONISTS £2.50 Jenny Beale. This book examines the overlap between feminist politics and trade unionism and shows that housework and childcare should concern all trade unionists. (Pluto Press 1982)

WOMEN AT WORK (1977) £2.20 Lindsey Mackie and Polly Pattullo. Examines the jobs that women do and why the pattern of women's employment is so different from that of men. Follows women through education training and the workplace. (Tavistock Womens Studies 1977)

LEWISHAM WOMEN AND EMPLOYMENT PROJECT: several project reports on women's employment. Unemployment and training in Lewisham £1 each. (Lewisham Women and Employment Project, 19 Deptford High Street, London SE8)

WOMEN, WORK AND TRADE UNION ORGANISATION 60p Shelley Adams and Judith Hunt. (WEA Studies Trade Unionists 1980)

WOMEN IN THE EIGHTIES 95p (Counter Information Services 1981)

JOB SHARING: improving the quality and availability of part-time work free (EOC)

JOB SHARING: guidelines for unions free (TUC)

WOMEN AND UNIONS

TUC CHARTER: EQUALITY FOR WOMEN WITHIN TRADE UNIONS free (TUC)

EQUAL OPPORTUNITIES: POSITIVE ACTION PROGRAMME 35p (TUC)

COLLECTIVE BARGAINING: ASSISTANCE FOR WORKING PARENTS 35p (TUC)

HEAR THIS BROTHER – WOMEN WORKERS AND TRADE UNION POWER £1.50 Anna Coote and Peter Kellner (New Statesman 1981)

SETTING UP A WORK PLACE NURSERY: a manual for employers and employees free (EOC)

JOB EVALUATION

JOB EVALUATION SCHEMES FREE OF BIAS free (EOC)
JOB EVALUATION AND MERIT RATING 25p (TUC)
JOB EVALUATION free (ACAS)
JOB EVALUATION REVIEW £5.00 (Income Data Services 1983)

EQUAL PAY ACT

AMENDING THE EQUALITY LAWS 95p Catherine Scorer and Ann Sedley (NCCL 1983)

EQUAL PAY FOR WORK OF EQUAL VALUE

EOC CONSULTATIVE DOCUMENT ON EQUAL PAY FOR WORK OF EQUAL VALUE free

COMMENTS ON DRAFT ORDER FOR EQUAL PAY FOR EQUAL VALUE by Northern Ireland EOC free

WOMEN AND JOB EVALUATION: the implications of the proposed amendment to the Equal Pay Act (Discussion Paper number 29 by TURU, Ruskin College Oxford)

LABOUR LAW IN IRELAND £3.30 Naomi Wayne (Kincora Press) (obtainable from ITGWU, 10 Palmerson Park, Dublin 6.)